THE SCIENTIFIC CASE FOR CREATION

by
HENRY M. MORRIS, Ph.D.

CLP PUBLISHERS
P.O. Box 15666
San Diego, California 92115

ISBN 0-89051-037-7

Library of Congress Card Catalog
Number 77-78019
Copyright © 1977

CLP PUBLISHERS

San Diego, California 92115

1st Printing July, 1977
2nd Printing October, 1977
3rd Printing, 1979
4th Printing, 1981

FOREWORD

This small book is intended to serve as a brief introduction to the broad field of scientific creationism. Intended primarily for scientists, teachers, and college students, the subject is treated solely from a scientific point of view, leaving the theological and Biblical implications of both evolution and creation to other studies. In spite of its theme, however (which does presuppose a certain minimal level of scientific background on the part of the reader for full understanding), an attempt has been made to enable even the general reader to follow the arguments and to appreciate the conclusions.

The discussion covers the following main arguments: (1) the basic laws of science show that evolution is impossible at present, while simultaneously pointing back to the necessity of an initial special creation of all things in the past; (2) the fossil record shows that evolution has not occurred in the past any more than it is occurring at present, and, furthermore, shows overwhelming evidence that the geologic column was formed rapidly in a recent worldwide flood, not slowly through many long geological ages; (3) the weight of the evidence provided by the earth's many physical processes is that the earth is very young, not nearly old enough for evolution to be a feasible explanation for the origin and development of things. The scientific model of origins that best fits all the available scientific data is that of a recent, supernatural creation of the universe and all its basic components by a transcendent Creator. The writer hopes this brief study will prove challenging to the reader and will encourage him or her to further consideration of this vital issue and all its implications.

Henry M. Morris, Ph.D.
San Diego, California
January, 1977

CONTENTS

Chapter 1
INTRODUCTION

For over a century, the uniformitarian-evolutionary model of earth history has dominated scientific thinking. During the past two decades, however, a revival of creationism and catastrophism has been gathering momentum, until today there are thousands of scientists who no longer believe in evolution. Many states have been considering whether to require creation as an alternative to evolution in science curricula. Debates between evolutionists and creationists—formal, structured scientific debates, that is—have taken place on dozens of university campuses in the past three years. Most of the students in the large audiences at these debates agreed that the creationist arguments were good ones.

What is the reason for this unexpected development? Many have dismissed it as a sociological or religious phenomenon, related somehow to postwar disenchantment with science, or to the modern revival of religious fundamentalism, or to rejection of the social and moral systems that are based on evolution. No doubt these phenomena are all related, but it is not obvious which are causes and which are effects.

The scientific creationists themselves are men and women who have acquired all the standard credentials of the scientist, but who maintain that creation explains the facts of science better than evolution does. To them it is not primarily a question of religion (after all, people can be religious and moral while still believing in evolution), but of science. They are convinced that the creation model correlates the scientific data more effectively. Although creationism is still a minority viewpoint among scientists, all scientists owe it to themselves and to society in general to keep an open mind. The majority belief is not always the correct belief, and what one believes about origins determines to a large degree what he believes about most other major issues in life.

Chapter 2
THE TWO MODELS

There are basically only two possible models of earth history, though there are variations within each. In the *evolution model,* the entire universe is considered to have evolved by natural processes into its present state of high organization and complexity. Since natural laws and processes are believed to operate uniformly, such evolutionary developments are interpreted in an over-all context of *uniformitarianism.*

The *creation model,* on the other hand, defines a period of special creation in the beginning, during which the basic systems of nature were brought into existence in completed, functioning form right from the start. Since "natural" processes do not accomplish such things at present, these creative processes must have been "supernatural" processes, requiring an omnipotent, transcendent Creator for their implementation. Once the Creator (whoever He may be) had completed the work of creation, the *creating* processes were terminated and replaced with *conserving* processes, to maintain the world and to enable it to accomplish its purpose.

In the evolutionary model, the universe in its present form began in a state of randomness and has been gradually becoming more ordered and complex over the ages, as illustrated in Figure 1.

In order for the complex structure of the universe to have been produced by present natural processes, tremendous aeons of time would have been required. Current estimates range up to 3×10^{10} (30 billion) years, with the earth evolving about 5×10^9 (5 billion) years ago.

The creation model (Figure 2), on the other hand, shows the universe created in perfect order during the creation period. Particles, chemicals, planets, stars, organisms, and people were all present from the start, so that long ages were not required for their development.

Although the universe was thereafter to be maintained by the continuing processes of conservation, it is conceivable that its "degree of order" would change. If so, however, the order could not increase (having begun in perfection); it could only decrease.

Unlike the evolution model, which permits both increases and decreases in order in the universe through natural processes (with the net effect being an increase), the

Figure 1. The Evolution Model

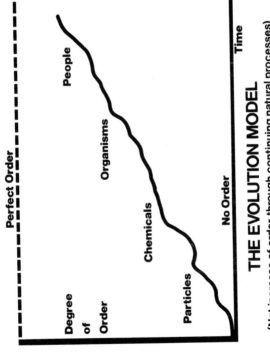

THE EVOLUTION MODEL

(Net increase of order through continuing natural processes)

Figure 2. The Creation Model

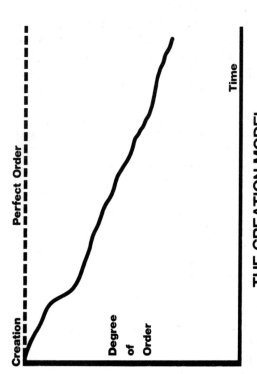

THE CREATION MODEL
(Net decrease of order following completed supernatural creation)

creation model allows only net decreases in order (for the universe as a whole) through natural processes, since only supernatural processes could generate net increases in order. The creation model stipulates nothing concerning the *rate* of decrease in order, however. This may be almost zero in times of peace and calm and very high during great catastrophes.

Many scientists may be surprised at the creationists' claim that the creation model is more effective than the evolution model in explaining scientific data. Several examples to illustrate this claim will be cited later.

In any case, everyone—both evolutionists and creationists—should recognize that neither model can be *proved* scientifically. As admitted by Matthews in the Foreword to the 1971 edition of Darwin's *Origin of Species:*

> "The fact of evolution is the backbone of biology, and biology is thus in the peculiar position of being a science founded on an unproved theory—is it then a science or a faith? Belief in the theory of evolution is thus exactly parallel to belief in special creation—both are concepts which believers know to be true but neither, up to the present, has been capable of proof."[1]

In a similar vein, Leon Harris has said:

"First, the axiomatic nature of the neo-Darwinian theory places the debate between evolutionists and creationists in a new perspective. Evolutionists have often challenged creationists to provide experimental proof that species have been fashioned *de novo*. Creationists have often demanded that evolutionists show how chance mutations can lead to adaptability, or to explain why natural selection has favored some species but not others with special adaptations, or why natural selection allows apparently detrimental organs to persist. We may now recognize that neither challenge is fair. If the neo-Darwinian theory is axiomatic, it is not valid for creationists to demand proof of the axioms, and it is not valid for evolutionists to dismiss special creation as unproved so long as it is stated as an axiom."[2]

Therefore, since we cannot repeat history, it is impossible to prove scientifically which model is correct. Creation is not taking place now, and thus it is not subject to experimental observation. Evolution takes place so slowly (in the sense of increasing order) that it could not be observed either, even if it were true.

Consequently, a decision as to which to believe must be made on the basis of which model explains the data better. Such a decision may well be largely subjective.

In any case, both evolutionists and creationists should be aware of the arguments and evidence for both models. To the extent that it is possible, the scientist should continually and consciously try to evaluate all new data that come to hand in light of both models.

Since every scientist is already familiar with the evolution model and is, therefore, accustomed to interpreting his data in an evolutionary framework, the balance of this study will concentrate on evidences favoring the creation model. Since there are only two possible models, and they are diametrically opposed, it is clear that evidence against evolution constitutes positive evidence for creation and evidence against creation is evidence for evolution. Of course, either model can be modified to accommodate any set of data, so that neither can be firmly proved or falsified. However, the model which fits the larger number of data with the smaller number of secondary modifications is the one which is more likely to be true.

Chapter 3
IS EVOLUTION POSSIBLE AT PRESENT?

If evolution is true, then there must be some innovational and integrative principle operating in the natural world which develops order out of randomness and higher order from lower order. Since, by uniformitarianism, this principle is still in effect, scientists should be able to observe and quantify it.

The creation model, on the other hand, suggests that there should be a conservational and disintegrative principle operating in nature. Since the total quantity of matter and energy, as well as the perfect degree of order, were created supernaturally in the beginning, we could not expect to see naturalistic processes of innovation and integration, as required by evolution, working today.

From the creation model, in fact, one would quickly predict two universal natural laws: (1) a law of conservation, tending to preserve the basic categories created in the beginning (laws of nature, matter, energy, basic kinds of organisms, etc.), in order to enable them to accomplish the purpose for which they were created; (2) a law of decay, tending to reduce the *available* matter, energy, kinds, etc., as the perfect order of the created cosmos runs down to disorder. As far as *changes* are concerned, one would expect from the creation model that there would be "horizontal" changes within limits (that is, energy conversions, variation within biologic kinds, etc.), and even "vertically-downward" changes in accordance with the law of decay (for example, mutations, wear, extinction, etc.), but never any *net* "vertically upward" changes, as required by evolution.

These two contrary sets of predictions from the two models should be testable in terms of structures and processes in the real world. It is noteworthy, then, that no one has ever *observed* any phenomenon requiring a universal principle of innovation or integration to explain it. Localized temporary phenomena of *apparent* increasing order (e.g., a growing organism) are only superficial, developing within broader systems of decreasing order which always "win out" in the end.

On the other hand, universal laws of conservation and decay *have* been observed. In fact, these principles are called the First and Second Laws of Thermodynamics—the law of conservation of mass-energy and the law of increasing entropy (or disorder). All scientific measurements ever made to date confirm the validity of these two laws. They govern all processes of any sort, so far as known. These laws of thermodynamics apply not only in physics and chemistry but also in biology and geology. Furthermore, there seem to be similar principles operating at the scale of living complexes. That is, "like begets like." Many varieties of dogs can be produced, but never can one breed a dog from some other *kind* of animal. The same restraint operates throughout the entire realm of life, so far as observations go. Similarly, certain organs in animals may atrophy and become "vestigial," or even entire kinds become extinct, but never do scientists observe "nascent" organs, or new kinds evolving.

The Second Law of Thermodynamics is especially significant in its support of the creation model and, correspondingly, its contradiction of the evolution model. Its nature and universality are well recognized:

> "As far as we know, all changes are in the direction of increasing entropy, of increasing disorder, of increasing randomness, of running down."[3]

But if the universe is now running down,

how did it get wound up in the first place? The most probable answer is creation. Note Figure 3.

During the period of observation, the total energy of the universe has, so far as known, remained unchanged but the available energy continually decreases; this "arrow of time" aims at an ultimate *heat death* of the universe, with the total energy still unchanged in quantity but totally unavailable for further work. The most probable extrapolation of the historic trends into the prehistoric period would follow the same curves, shown as dotted lines on Figure 3. The two curves meet at T_0, the time when the total energy was totally available. This point of discontinuity also denotes the time when there presumably was perfect order in the universe.

The Second Law implies that, if present processes continue, the universe will become completely "dead" in time. If it were *infinitely* old, it would already be dead. Thus, in its present form, it must have had a beginning! The First Law, however, indicates that it could not have created itself. It must, therefore, have been created by a Creator outside itself and by processes of creation which are not now occurring, exactly as the creation model postulates.

This evidence does not necessarily *prove* creation to be true. It is conceivable that a

Figure 3. Implications of Laws
of Thermodynamics

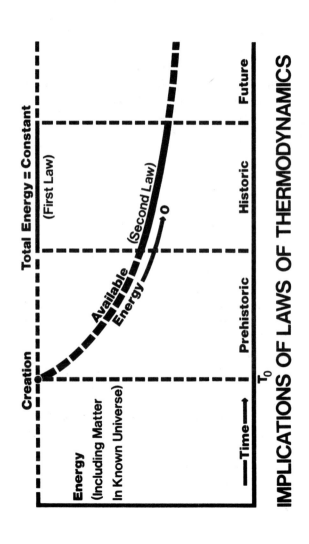

IMPLICATIONS OF LAWS OF THERMODYNAMICS

naturalistic integrative process might have occurred in the time before time T_0, or that such a process might even today be occurring in that part of the universe outside the *known* universe. In *observable* space and time, however, there is no such thing. Science is what we *see,* and we see only a universal disintegrative process pointing back to an initial creation.

Not only does the Second Law point back to creation; it also directly contradicts evolution. Systems do not naturally go toward higher order, but toward lower order. Evolution requires a universal principle of upward change; the entropy law is a universal principle of downward change. If language is meaningful, evolution and the Second Law cannot both be true. The Second Law, however, has been confirmed by all sorts of scientific tests, while evolution is a model not even capable of being tested scientifically. If one must make a choice, it would seem better to go with science!

Even though evolution and entropy cannot both be universal laws, many evolutionists insist that evolution could take place locally and temporarily. The earth is an open system, and there is energy enough from the sun to sustain evolution during the geologic ages, even if the process will eventually cease when the sun dies.

Creationists reply that merely having an

open system and energy available from the sun does not automatically generate higher order in that system. All *real* systems are open systems and are open in one way or another to the sun's energy, but most such systems normally proceed to lower degrees of order in accord with the law of entropy.

The question is: What conditions must be satisfied to cause any finite system to advance to a higher degree of order, when the universe as a whole is decreasing in order? Careful analysis of all types of local systems of increasing order (e.g., seed growing into a tree, building being constructed out of bricks and other components) shows that at least four criteria must be fulfilled in every case. These are outlined on Figure 4.

As far as the earth is concerned, *every* real system is an open system and is open either directly or indirectly to the sun's energy. Yet no system shows an increasing order unless it also possesses a highly specific program to direct its growth and a complex mechanism (or "motor," or "membrane") to convert the sun's energy into the specific work of building its growth. The best examples are living systems and artificial systems. As noted in Figure 4, a typical living system and a typical artificial system do meet these criteria. One case often cited—formation of a crystal out of a cooling liquid—is not a valid example, however, since the energy

Figure 4. Criteria for Increasing Order

CRITERIA	SYSTEM	
	GROWING PLANT	BUILDING CONSTRUCTION
1. Open System	Seed	Materials
2. Available Energy	Sun	Sun
3. Directing Program	Genetic Code	Blueprint
4. Conversion Mechanism	Photosynthesis	Workmen

Criteria for Increasing Order

or information contained in the liquid is higher than in the crystal which develops from it. In any case, the program and the mechanism required to increase the order in a system must have been provided somehow beforehand, and no accidental or random phenomenon is capable of generating either such a program or such a mechanism.

With this in mind, the question is whether the biosphere as a whole can evolve into higher order. Figure 5 outlines the problem.

Every stage of true organic evolution represents an increase in order of a living system. In each case, the system is an open system with energy available in the form of sunlight. The problem is: What are the programs and the mechanisms? What is the pre-existing program that directs the inorganic chemicals of the primeval soup how to become the first replicating chemicals? As yet there is no answer. Also, what is the complex energy converter that transforms the solar energy into the infinitely intricate structures required for life?

Once simple life has appeared, however, is it possible for a population of simple organisms to be transformed into a population of more complex organisms? What is the conversion mechanism that converts the sun's energy into the specific work required to build up this more complex

Figure 5. Absence of Ordering Criteria in Evolution

CRITERIA TO BE SATISFIED	S Y S T E M	
	FIRST LIVING CELL	POPULATION OF COMPLEX ORGANISMS
Open System	Complex Inanimate Molecule	Population of Simple Organisms
Available Energy	Sun	Sun
Directing Program	None	None (Natural Selection?)
Conversion Mechanism	None	None (Mutations?)

Absence of Ordering Criteria in Evolution

system? The phenomenon of mutation is a response to environmental radiations, of course, but never do genes mutate in such a way as to increase the *order* of the genetic system. Mutations are random changes and, *so far as all observations go,* random changes in ordered systems inevitably decrease the order in those systems. Also, what is the directing program that instructs a population of worms to develop themselves into a population of, say, crocodiles? Natural selection serves as a conservational "program," weeding out harmful mutations, but it cannot specify the development of more complex systems.

Thus, it seems that evolution in the vertically upward sense is impossible in the light of the Second Law of Thermodynamics. If even such a simple system as a seed requires a previously available program and mechanism (genetic code and photosynthesis) to grow in complexity, much more must this be true of the gigantic space-time continuum which constitutes the supposedly evolving biosphere.

Evolutionists, for the most part, have ignored this problem. A few evolutionists, mostly in the physical sciences, have recognized it and are trying to solve it—so far, mainly by speculative suggestions. Prigogine, for example, proposes that "fluctuations" or "instabilities" in what he calls "dissipative structures" can generate higher order in an open system. However, he acknowledges that there is no evidence that life originated by any such means.

"The probability that at ordinary temperatures a macroscopic number of molecules is assembled to give rise to the highly ordered structures and to the coordinated functions characterizing living organisms is vanishingly small. The idea of spontaneous generation of life in its present form is therefore highly improbable, even on the scale of the billions of years during which prebiotic evolution occurred."[4]

In another paper Prigogine holds out some hope that his theory may eventually be able to provide the missing ordering mechanism. He cautions, however:

"But it is not just one instability that makes it possible to cross the threshold between life and non-life; it is, rather a succession of instabilities of which we are only now beginning to identify certain stages."[5]

It is the same old problem. How can an increase of order (or "information") be produced in a system (whether open or closed) by any kind of random process? All experience, as well as any probabilistic or mathematical analysis, indicates that *random* changes lead only to a *decrease* of order.

David Layzer, of Harvard, has also attempted to deal with this problem. He first redefines "time's arrow" (a term coined for the Second Law by Sir Arthur Eddington) in terms of two arrows, one pointing up and one pointing down:

"The processes that define the historical and the thermodynamic arrows of time generate information and entropy, respectively."[6]

By the "historical arrow", Layzer means the evolutionary process, which presumably generates a higher and higher degree of "information" (or "order" or "complexity") in the world. This can only be done at the cost of decreasing entropy.

"Thus a gain of information is always compensated for by an equal loss of entropy."[7]

However, the "thermodynamic arrow" defines entropy as always increasing. Layzer, in effect, has restated the problem, but he hasn't solved it. That is, just *how* is this increasing information generated at the cost of a loss of entropy? What is the code that directs it and where is the mechanism that actuates it? Without these, the naturally increasing entropy simply precludes an increase of information. The vacuous statement that "the earth is an open system" is no answer. Charles Smith recognizes this fact, though understating its significance, as follows:

"This explanation, however, is not completely satisfying, because it still leaves the problem of how or why the ordering process has arisen (an apparent lowering of the entropy), and a number of scientists have wrestled with this issue.

"Bertalanffy (1968) called the relation between irreversible thermodynamics and information theory one of the most fundamental unsolved problems in biology. I would go further and include the problem of meaning and value."[8]

As observed in Figure 6, this "fundamental unsolved problem in biology" is essentially a statement of the two contradictory predictions of change postulated by the creation and evolution models.

It should be remembered that the Second Law is a proved law of science (to the extent there can be such a thing), whereas Evolution is a model which is not only unproved but untestable.

Even if Prigogine or other workers in this field were ever able to conceive a possible code and mechanism by which evolutionary increases in order might be produced in spite of a universe of increasing entropy, the Evolution Model still would not be as effective as the Creation

Figure 6. Time's Arrows—
Evolution versus Science

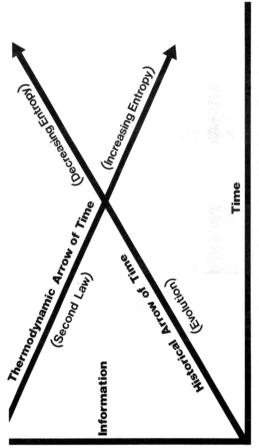

TIME'S ARROWS–EVOLUTION VS. SCIENCE

Model. The Evolution Model, by any such secondary modification and extension, might then perhaps be *harmonized* with the Second Law, but it could never predict it. The Creation Model, however *predicts* the Second Law. As far as the laws of science at present are concerned, evolution seems to be impossible.

Chapter 4
DID EVOLUTION
OCCUR IN THE PAST?

Evolution on any significant scale seems to be impossible at present, in light of the empirically proved Second Law of Thermodynamics. Is it possible, however, that conditions were different in past ages, so that evolution could have occurred throughout the geological ages, even though we cannot see how it could be occurring at present?

There are no records of vertically upward evolution occurring since the beginning of written history, so it is necessary to study records of the pre-history of the earth to answer this question. These records are found almost exclusively in the rocks of the earth's crust, especially the fossil-bearing sedimentary rocks that have been laid down above its "basement complex" of primeval crystalline rocks—that is, in the "geologic column."

It is well known that the local geologic

column at any given place is usually quite different from that at any other place. However, these all are summed to fit somewhere in the standard geologic time table, which is believed by evolutionists to constitute the lithic record of all the earth's evolutionary geological ages, from the Precambrian up to the Recent. The physical interpretation of the processes that formed these rocks is based on the principle of *uniformitarianism*—that is, the principle that present laws and processes, operating esentially as they do at present, are sufficient to account for all these great rock systems.

If the Evolution Model is correct, present processes have produced not only the rocks but also the various forms of life preserved as fossils in the rocks. Thus, uniformitarianism is an essential component of the model. These processes operate slowly—in fact, so slowly in the case of vertically upward evolutionary changes that we cannot see them operating at all in the present historical period. Thus a tremendous—almost infinite—span of time is necessary for evolution to be feasible by any natural process.

Similarly, if evolution was operating through these past geological ages, then all the present complex forms of life were slowly developing from primeval simple forms of life, and this should be documented by the fossils found in the rock record of these ages. The fossil record should show an abundance of intermediate, transitional forms of plants and animals, showing how the various phyla, classes, orders, and families developed through the ages.

The Creation Model, on the other hand, postulates that all the basic kinds* of plants and animals were specially created and did not evolve from other kinds at all. Consequently the Creationist predicts that no transitional sequences (except within the *kind*) will ever be found, either in the present array of organisms or in the fossil record.

That this prediction is borne out in the present assemblage of plants and animals is obvious to all. If it were not so, it would not even be possible to have a taxonomic system—one could never determine the dividing lines between similar organisms.

"In other words, the living world is not a single array of individuals in which any two variants are connected by unbroken series of intergrades, but

---

*The term "kind" is used to denote the originally created entity, within which variation could take place. The entities of the Linnaean system (species, genera, families, orders, etc.), are, of course, arbitrary human taxonomic inventions and are often changed. Though it is impossible to precisely equate one of these with the "kind", it may be that the "family" is a good approximation.

an array of more or less distinct-
ly separate arrays, in-
termediates between which are
absent or rare."[9]

This in itself is strange. It would be much
better confirmation of the Evolution Model
if all variants *were* connected by unbroken
series of intergrades. Creationists would be
hard pressed to explain *that* sort of thing.
As it stands, however, the present array of
organisms (abundant variation within
limited categories, clear-cut gaps between
categories) fits precisely the expectations
of the Creation Model.

The fossil record is the key test,
however. Transitional series *must* have
existed in the past, if evolution is true, and
the fossil record should reveal at least
some of these.

The fact is, however, that no such transitional series—or even occasional transitional forms—have ever been found in the
fossil record. The leading paleontologist,
George G. Simpson, recognizes this, as
does another prominent paleontologist (and
student of Simpson's) David Kitts.

". . . every paleontologist
knows, that *most* new species,
genera, and families, and that
nearly all categories above the
level of families, appear in the
record suddenly and are not led
up to by known, gradual, completely continuous transitional
sequences."[10]

"Despite the bright promise that paleontology provides a means of 'seeing' evolution, it has presented some nasty difficulties for evolutionists, the most notorious of which is the presence of 'gaps' in the fossil record. Evolution requires intermediate forms between species and paleontology does not provide them. The gaps must therefore be a contingent feature of the record."[11]

Still more recently, two University of California scientists add their testimony:

"The abrupt appearance of higher taxa in the fossil record has been a perennial puzzle. Not only do characteristic and distinctive remains of phyla appear suddenly, without known ancestors, but several classes of a phylum, orders of a class, and so on, commonly appear at approximately the same time, without known intermediates."[12]

The phenomenon of the ubiquitous absence of transitional forms in the fossil record could be documented at great length. Evolutionists have suggested various explanations—the inadequacy of the fossil record, explosive evolution in small populations, and others. All such explanations are based upon the *absence* of evidence, a strange situation in science. Actual fossils of transitional forms would be much better evidence of evolution than their absence!

The Creation Model, on the other hand, is not embarrassed by these gaps in the fossil record. Evolutionists have to try to *explain* the gaps, whereas the gaps are precisely predicted from the Creation Model.

There is, therefore, no evidence that the laws of nature were different in the past than they are at present. The Second Law of Thermodynamics seems to prevent upward evolutionary change in the present, and it apparently did the same in the past.

If, therefore, the major groups of plants and animals (that is, the "kinds") were specially created, the uniformitarian assumption is not valid as an explanation of their origin. There would be no need, then, to postulate a great age for the earth, as far as the origin of life and the various kinds of life are concerned. Furthermore, uniformitarianism may also be questionable as an explanation of the origin and history of the earth. Perhaps the geologic column was not formed slowly over long ages by uniformitarian processes, but rapidly, in one age, by cataclysmic processes. After all, there is no way to *prove* prehistoric uniformitarianism, since no scientific observers were present in the prehistoric past.

Most people do not realize that the very

existence of the long geological ages is based on the assumption of evolution. It is well known that the geologic ages are identified and dated solely by the fossils found in the sediments formed in those ages. Rocks of all types, minerals of all types, structures of all types, are found in rocks of all ages. The only thing different about them in the different "ages" is their assemblage of fossils. Radiometric dating applies strictly only to igneous formations and is notoriously unreliable, as discussed in the next section. Not even vertical superposition is definitive, since "old" formations are very often found superposed on "young" formations, frequently with no actual physical evidence of any phenomenon that might have reversed the original order of deposition. In the last analysis, the final and definitive criterion of geologic age is that of index fossils.

But how do such fossils determine the age of a rock? Dr. H. D. Hedberg, then president of the Geological Society of America, answers:

> ". . . fossils have furnished, through their record of the evolution of life on this planet, an amazingly effective key to the relative positioning of strata in widely separated regions and from continent to continent."[13]

The leading European paleontologist likewise says:

"The only chronometric scale applicable in geologic history for that stratigraphic classification of rocks and for dating geologic events exactly is furnished by the fossils. Owing to the irreversibility of evolution, they offer an unambiguous time-scale for relative age determinations and for worldwide correlations of rocks."[14]

That is, since evolution takes place worldwide, rocks containing fossils representing a certain stage of evolution are assumed to have been formed during the age when that evolutionary stage was attained. This would certainly be the best way of dating rocks, if we knew for certain—say, by divine revelation—that evolution were true.

But this is the very question. If the Creation Model is a better model than the Evolution Model, as creationists believe, then evolution is *not* true, and there is no way to distinguish one geologic age from another. In fact, they may all be the *same* age!

This criticism of the Evolution Model is all the more cogent in light of the fact that most evolutionists think the fossil record is the best evidence for evolution. As Dunbar says:

". . . fossils provide the only historical, documentary evidence that life has evolved from simpler to more and more complex forms."[15]

How can the fossil sequence prove evolution if the rocks containing the fossils have been dated by those fossils on the basis of the assumed stage of evolution of those same fossils? This is pure circular reasoning, based on the arbitrary assumption that the Evolution Model is true. Some evolutionists recognize this problem. David Kitts, of the University of Oklahoma, admits:

"But the danger of circularity is still present. For most biologists the strongest reason for accepting the evolutionary hypothesis is their acceptance of some theory that entails it. There is another difficulty. The temporal ordering of biological events beyond the local section may critically involve paleontological correlation, which necessarily presupposes the non-repeatability of organic events in geologic history. There are various justifications for this assumption but for almost all contemporary paleontologists it rests upon the acceptance of the evolutionary hypothesis."[16]

Similarly, Ronald West, at Kansas State, says:

"Contrary to what most scientists write, the fossil record does not support the Darwinian theory of evolution because it is this theory (there are several) which we use to interpret the fossil record. By doing so, we are guilty of circular reasoning if we then say the fossil record supports this theory."[17]

There seems really no objective reason why the entire range of organic life preserved in the fossils could not have been living concurrently in one age. If so, it is reasonable to give serious consideration to a return to *catastrophism,* rather than uniformitarianism, as the explanation of the geologic column. In this model, the great beds of sedimentary rocks were formed mainly by a great worldwide Deluge, as believed by the founding fathers of geology (Steno, Woodward, *et al*) before the rise of the uniformitarians (Hutton, Lyell, Darwin).

This Flood Model of geology can be examined in terms of five predictions:

(1) most or all formations should be explainable in terms of catastrophic intensities of the processes which formed them;

(2) evidence should exist of continuous deposition, without significant time gaps, of the entire geologic column;

(3) the order of deposition in any local column should usually be in terms of increasing mobility and the elevation of ecological habitat of the organisms preserved as fossils in that column;

(4) the order of deposition in any given formation should usually be the order implied by the hydraulic processes producing it as a single depositional unit;

(5) because of the cataclysmic and complex geophysical phenomena associated with a worldwide flood, there would be occasional exceptions to the order of fossil deposition specified as "usual" in predictions (4) and (5).

Now even if one prefers to believe in the uniformitarian interpretation of geology, he should recognize that each of the five predictions above are fulfilled in the actual facts of geology. In the first place, it has become obvious in recent years that normal, slow processes of sedimentation, tectonism, volcanism, etc., could never produce the formations and structures found in the earth's crust, not to mention the coal, oil, and metal deposits. Dr. Derek Ager, Head of the Geology Department at Swansea University in England, has recently published an entire book demonstrating that every formation requires a catastrophic explanation. He concludes his book as follows:

"In other words, the history of any one part of the earth, like the life of a soldier, consists of long periods of boredom and short periods of terror."[18]

That is, everything we can actually see in the geologic column is the result of geologic catastrophes. There is no visible evidence of the supposed vast periods of time in between. Dr. Ager does not believe in a worldwide cataclysm, but rather in a succession of regional catastrophes, each separated from the next by a long time gap of unknown duration. Such time gaps presumably were times of slow erosion, marked by unconformities in the geologic column.

In the second place, however, it should be emphasized that there are no worldwide unconformities and therefore no worldwide time gaps in the column. That is, formation A may be separated from formation B in locality "1" by a clear unconformity, whereas it rests conformably on the same formation in locality "2", as sketched in Figure 7. There may have been a period of uplift and erosion in region "1", while deposition was continuous in region "2".

In any case, whatever the specific physical sequences may have been, there is no worldwide unconformity, and thus no worldwide time gap.

Figure 7. Limited Extent of Unconformities

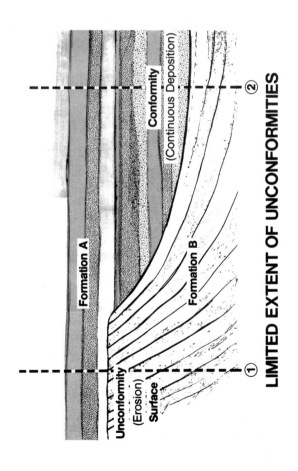

LIMITED EXTENT OF UNCONFORMITIES

> "In the early history of stratigraphy, unconformities were overestimated in that they were believed to represent coeval disastrophism over areas of infinitely wide extent."[19]

The ideas of worldwide "revolutions" and mountain-building upheavals at the end of each geological epoch are still reflected in the terminology of the standard geologic time-table, but they correspond to no real chronology in the real geologic column.

> "Many unconformity bounded units are considered to be chronostratigraphic units in spite of the fact that unconformity surfaces inevitably cut across isochronous horizons and hence cannot be true chronostratigraphic boundaries."[20]

The obvious conclusion is that there is no clear physically demarked worldwide time boundary anywhere in the geologic column. That can only mean that, since each unit in the column was deposited rapidly, as already noted, the entire column was formed rapidly. The entire sedimentary crust, therefore, fits the prediction of the Flood Model—continuous, cataclysmic hydraulic sedimentary activity throughout the column.

The last three predictions of the Flood Model are obviously confirmed, since the order of deposition which they suggest for the fossils is from the simpler on the bottom to the complex on top (with occasional exceptions), and it is this very order which has been appropriated by the evolutionist in support of his own model. The occasional exceptions (inverted sequences in the geologic column and fossils from different "ages" in the same formation) are easy enough to understand in a cataclysmic Deluge, but very difficult to explain in terms of simple uniformitarianism.

The Flood Model of the earth's geologic crust, as a supplement and corollary of the basic Creation Model of origins (although it cannot be scientifically proved, since one cannot repeat history), does fit all the facts at least as well as the Evolution-Uniformitarian Model, with fewer unsolved problems, and so should be seriously considered by scientists.

Chapter 5
IS THE EARTH REALLY OLD
. . . OR JUST TIRED?

If the Creation-Flood Model is valid, then there is no real reason to think the earth is much older than mankind and the beginning of human history. The hypothetical billions of years usually assumed are only necessary to accommodate evolution and the uniformitarian interpretation of the geologic column. The Creation Model can, therefore, take a serious look at the chronometric implications of *all* of earth's processes, not only the three or four processes that can be interpreted to yield ages old enough to allow for evolution.

In accordance with the Second Law of Thermodynamics, all systems are decaying. The decay rate for each physical quantity varies, of course, with the particular process and with all the parameters in the function defining the process. In general, a decay function tends to plot up as an exponential curve of some sort—falling off rapidly at first, then gradually attenuating and approaching zero asymptotically. At any point along the curve, if an external interruption (catastrophe) affects the process, the decay may speed up abnormally for a period, then settle back down to a normal decay rate.

In some decay functions, the half-life of the decaying quantity is constant. Radioactive minerals and certain other systems (though certainly not all systems) appear to decay in this fashion. Many follow a simple exponential decay. Some may even decay linearly, though these are rare.

In most cases (note Fig. 8), the decaying quantity dissipates rapidly at first, attenuating later. It would usually be wrong to calculate a time duration on the assumption of linear dissipation with time, as this would almost invariably give too great an age. It is doubtful even that systems which are believed to decay with a uniform half-life have maintained even *that* quasi-uniform decay in the past.

If, for example, there has been some kind of traumatic environmental change in the past (catastrophe), then the parameters in its environment would have also accelerated its decay rate, again resulting in too large an "apparent age" of the system if calculated on the assumption of uniformity.

There are other effects which can discredit an age calculation also, to which

Figure 8. Exponential Decay of Physical Quantity

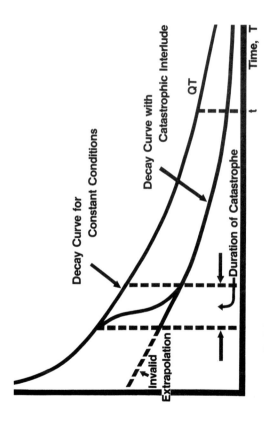

radiometric systems are particularly vulnerable (unknown initial conditions, extraneous alterations, etc.). Consider, in general, any system in which the quantities of its components are changing with time, as in Fig. 9.

There are innumerable natural systems in the world and all change with time. Therefore, any such system could be used as a chronometer if the necessary information on it can be obtained.

In the simple system sketched in Fig. 9, only two components are present, with reactions taking place such that component A is changing into component B, at a certain rate r at a certain time t. Although the system is confined within boundaries, no boundaries are impenetrable, so it is possible that increments are being added to either component from outside the system. Similarly, increments of either component may somehow escape the system. This process has been going on for some unknown time, and it is assumed that, when it started, components A and B had initial magnitudes A_0 and B_0.

If the quantities A_T and B_T are measured at some time T, the value of T (that is, the "apparent age" of the system, or at least the time since the changes began to occur in the system) can be calculated as shown in Fig. 10.

Examination of equations (1), (2), and (3) indicates the idealistic nature of such

Figure 9. Natural System Changing with Time

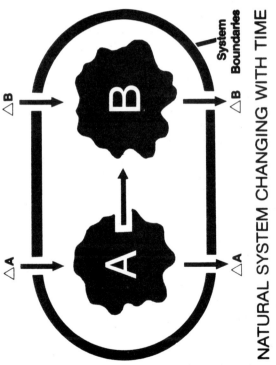

NATURAL SYSTEM CHANGING WITH TIME

Figure 10. Calculation of Apparent Age in a Changing System

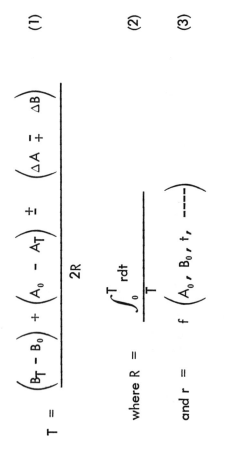

$$T = \frac{\left(B_T - B_0\right) + \left(A_0 - A_T\right) \pm \left(\Delta A \mp \Delta B\right)}{2R} \qquad (1)$$

$$\text{where } R = \frac{\int_0^T r\,dt}{T} \qquad (2)$$

$$\text{and } r = f\left(A_0, B_0, t, ----\right) \qquad (3)$$

Calculation of Apparent Age in a Changing System

calculations. The only quantities actually measureable are A_T, B_T, and r_T (the reaction rate at the time T). Equation (1), therefore, contains five unknowns and is impossible to solve unless all five of these are arbitrarily assumed. One of them, R, can be calculated from equation (2) if function (3) is known, but the latter involves still other unknowns.

The usual procedure in geochronometric calculations is to make the following assumptions, as listed on Fig. 11.

With these assumptions, it is now possible to make a calculation of apparent age from equation (1), replacing its five unknowns with the values assumed from equations (4) through (9). The result is the simple expression for T shown on Fig. 12 (more complex, of course, if other assumptions are made). The implicit meanings of the assumptions are also tabulated on Fig. 12.

With such unrealistic assumptions, one might just as well pick the age he wants in the first place, and then modify the assumptions until the apparent age agrees with his wishes. As a matter of fact, this is what evolutionists do, in effect, when they arbitrarily reject all chronometers and calculations which yield young ages for the earth or its different systems. There is nothing scientifically dishonest about this. Since all such calculations depend upon these arbitrary assumptions anyhow, it is

Figure 11. Required Assumptions for Age Calculation

1.	Assume r_T = constant = R	(4)
	(or some other specific functional relation)	(5)
2.	Assume $\Delta A = 0$ (or other arbitrary value)	(6)
3.	Assume $\Delta B = 0$ (or other arbitrary value)	(7)
4.	Assume $B_0 = 0$ (or other arbitrary value)	(8)
5.	Assume $A_0 = B_T + A_T - B_0$ (conservation of mass)	(9)

Required Assumptions for Age Calculation

Figure 12. Simplified Calculation
of Apparent Age

$$T = \frac{B_T - B_0}{r_T} = \frac{B_T}{r_T} \qquad (10)$$

Assumptions

1. Uniformitarianism (highly improbable)
2. Isolated System (non-existent)
3. Known Initial Conditions (indeterminable)
4. Conservation of Mass (valid)

Simplified Calculation of Apparent Age

logical for them to pick those which agree with their basic axiom of evolution. That is, this is scientifically honest if—but only if—they recognize and acknowledge that the entire calculation depends flatly on their arbitrary belief in evolution, which demands an immensity of time.

It is equally legitimate for creationists to calculate apparent ages using assumptions which agree with their belief in special creation, provided they acknowledge *that* fact.

As a matter of fact, it is very interesting that even on the basis of the usual uniformitarian-evolutionary assumptions (as listed on Figs. 11 and 12), there are far more chronometers that yield a young age for the earth than yield an old age. That is, if one analyzes any process of worldwide change (e.g., fall of extra-terrestrial material on the earth, erosion of lands, influx of chemicals into the ocean, etc.) and then makes the standard evolutionary assumptions (initial boundary values of zero, uniformity of process rates, closed system), he will find that practically all such calculations yield a terrestrial age of far less than a billion years. They will all give *different* values, for the obvious reason that the assumptions are in error by varying amounts in the various calculations. A number of such "ages" are shown on Table I. (See page 55).

There are 70 types of calculations listed

in Table I, all of them independent of each other and all applying essentially to the entire earth, or one of its major components or to the solar system. All give ages far too young to accommodate the Evolution Model. All are based on the same types of calculations and assumptions used by evolutionists on the very few systems (uranium, potassium, rubidium) whose radioactive decay seems to indicate ages in the billions of years. As noted in items 21 and 22 in Table I, even these methods (when based on real empirical evidence) yield young ages.

The most obvious characteristic of the values listed in the table is their extreme variability—all the way from 100 years to 500,000,000 years. This variability, of course, simply reflects the errors in the fundamental uniformitarian assumptions.

Nevertheless, all things considered, it seems that those ages on the low end of the spectrum are likely to be more accurate than those on the high end. This conclusion follows from the obvious fact that: (1) they are less likely to have been affected by initial concentrations or positions other than "zero"; (2) the assumption that the system was a "closed system" is more likely to be valid for a short time than for a long time; (3) the assumption that the process rate was constant is also more likely to be valid for a short time than for a long time.

Thus, it is concluded that the weight of all

the scientific evidence favors the view that the earth is quite young, far too young for life and man to have arisen by an evolutionary process. The origin of all things by special creation—already necessitated by many other scientific considerations—is therefore also indicated by chronometric data.

There is one other important point relative to chronology. While the Evolution Model requires a long chronology to be feasible, the Creation Model does not necessarily require a short chronology. Even if the earth were billions of years old, the basic arguments supporting creationism (stability of kinds, gaps between kinds, entropy principle, etc.) are not changed. In fact, the entropy law indicates that the older the universe, the less likely that anything could evolve toward higher order. The true arrow of time points down, with systems going toward lower order.

As a matter of fact, when this thermodynamic principle is stated in terms of probabilities, it is apparent that not even 30 billion years (the currently assumed age of the universe) would be sufficient for random processes to produce the simplest imaginable replicating system anywhere in the universe.

To investigate this situation, assume that the known universe (5×10^9 light-years radius) is crammed with tiny particles of

TABLE I

Uniformitarian Estimates—Age of the Earth

(Unless otherwise indicated, based on standard assumptions of (1) zero initial "daughter" component; (2) closed system; (3) uniform rate)

	Process	Indicated Age of Earth	Reference
1.	Decay of earth's magnetic field	10,000 years	21
2.	Influx of radiocarbon to the earth system	10,000 years	22
3.	Influx of meteoritic dust from space	too small to calculate	23
4.	Efflux of Helium-4 into the atmosphere	1,750-175,000 years	24
5.	Development of total human population	4,000 years	25
6.	Influx of uranium to the ocean via rivers	10,000-100,000 years	24
7.	Influx of sediment to the ocean via rivers	30,000,000 years	26
8.	Erosion of sediment from continents	14,000,000 years	26
9.	Leaching of sodium from continents	32,000,000 years	27
10.	Leaching of chlorine from continents	1,000,000 years	27
11.	Leacing of calcium from continents	12,000,000 years	27
12.	Influx of carbonate to the ocean	100,000 years	27
13.	Influx of sulphate to the ocean	10,000,000 years	27

55

	Process	Indicated Age of Earth	Reference
14.	Influx of chlorine to the ocean	164,000,000 years	27
15.	Influx of calcium to the ocean	1,000,000 years	27
16.	Efflux of oil from traps by fluid pressure	10,000-100,000 years	28
17.	Formation of radiogenic lead by neutron capture	too small to measure	28
18.	Formation of radiogenic strontium by neutron capture	too small to measure	28
19.	Decay of natural remanent paleomagnetism	100,000 years	28
20.	Decay of C-14 in pre-Cambrian wood	4,000 years	28
21.	Decay of uranium with initial lead	too small to measure	29
22.	Decay of potassium with entrapped argon	too small to measure	29
23.	Influx of juvenile water to oceans	340,000,000 years	30
24.	Influx of magma from mantle to form crust	500,000,000 years	30
25.	Growth of active coral reefs	10,000 years	30
26.	Growth of oldest living part of biosphere	5,000 years	30
27.	Origin of human civilizations	5,000 years	30

57

	Process	Indicated Age of Earth	Reference
47.	Influx of silicon to the ocean via rivers	8,000 years	41
48.	Influx of potassium to the ocean via rivers	11,000,000 years	41
49.	Influx of copper to the ocean via rivers	50,000 years	41
50.	Influx of gold to the ocean via rivers	560,000 years	41
51.	Influx of silver to the ocean via rivers	2,100,000 years	41
52.	Influx of mercury to the ocean via rivers	42,000 years	41
53.	Influx of lead to the ocean via rivers	2,000 years	41
54.	Influx of tin to the ocean via rivers	100,000 years	41
55.	Influx of aluminum to the ocean via rivers	100 years	41
56.	Influx of lithium into ocean via rivers	20,000,000 years	41
57.	Influx of titanium into ocean via rivers	160 years	41
58.	Influx of chromium into ocean via rivers	350 years	41
59.	Influx of manganese into ocean via rivers	1,400 years	41
60.	Influx of iron into ocean via rivers	140 years	41
61.	Influx of cobalt into ocean via rivers	18,000 years	41
62.	Influx of zinc into ocean via rivers	180,000 years	41

63.	Influx of rubidium into ocean via rivers	270,000 years	41
64.	Influx of strontium into ocean via rivers	19,000,000 years	41
65.	Influx of bismuth into ocean via rivers	45,000 years	41
66.	Influx of thorium into ocean via rivers	350 years	41
67.	Influx of antimony into ocean via rivers	350,000 years	41
68.	Influx of tungsten into ocean via rivers	1,000 years	41
69.	Influx of barium into ocean via rivers	84,000 years	41
70.	Influx of molybdenum into ocean via rivers	500,000 years	41

the size of an electron, the smallest known particle in existence. It has been estimated that 10^{80} such particles exist in the universe, but if there were no empty space, approximately 10^{130} particles conceivably could exist there. Every structure, every process, every system, every "event" in the universe must consist of these particles, in various combinations and interchanges.

If, to be extremely liberal, we assume that each particle can take part in 10^{20} (that is a hundred billion billion) events each second, and then allow 10^{20} seconds of cosmic history (this would correspond to 3000 billion years, or 100 times the current estimate of the age of the universe), then the greatest conceivable number of separate events that could ever take place in all of space and time would be

$$10^{130} \times 10^{20} \times 10^{20} = 10^{170} \text{ events.}$$

Now, in order for life to appear, one of these events (or some combination of them) must bring a number of these particles together in a system containing enough order (or stored information) to enable it to make a copy of itself. This system must be produced by chance, of course, since presumably no Creator or Designer is available to plan and direct the assemblage of all this information.

The problem is, however, that any living cell or any new organ to be added to an existing animal—even the simplest imaginable replicating system—would have to contain far more stored information than represented even by such a gigantic number as 10^{170}. A leading information scientist, Marcel Golay, [42] calculates the odds against such a system organizing itself randomly as 10^{450} to 1. Other studies [43, 44, 45] have been made attempting to get a similar measure, but all calculate a much higher state of ordered information and improbability even than this.

If we take Golay's figure, giving the Evolution Model all possible benefit of the doubt, the odds against any accidental ordering of particles into a replicating system is at least 10^{450} to 1. This is so whether it all happens in one event or in a series of connected events. As a matter of fact, Golay calculated the figure on the assumption that it was accomplished by a series of 1,500 successive events, each with a probability of ½ (Note that $2^{1500}=10^{450}$.) The probability would be much lower if it had to be accomplished in a single chance event.

It is very generous, therefore, to conclude that the probability of the simplest conceivable replicating system arising by chance just once in all the universe, in all time is:

$$\frac{10^{170}}{10^{450}} = \frac{1}{10^{280}}$$

This calculation is summarized in Figure 13.

When the probability of occurrence of any event is smaller than one out of the number of events that could ever possibly occur—that is, as discussed above, less than $1/10^{170}$, then the probability of its occurrence is considered to be zero. Consequently, it is concluded that the chance origin of life is absolutely impossible. Life can only be explained by special creation.

It is hardly surprising, therefore, that biochemists have found it so difficult to synthesize living systems from non-living chemicals, or that space scientists are unable to find evidence of extra-terrestrial life. Life is not an accident, nor even something that can be fabricated by clever men. All the evidence supports the Creation Model on this. Life must have been specially created!

The objection is sometimes posed that, even if the probability of a living system is 10^{-280}, every other specific combination of particles might also have a similar probability of occurrence, so that one is just as likely as another. There even may be other combinations than the one with which we are familiar on earth that might turn out to be living.

Such a statement overlooks the fact that, in any group of particles, there are many more meaningless combinations than

Figure 13. Number of Events in Space and Time; Probability of Chance Origin of Life

Number of Events in Space and Time

Number of possible particles in universe $= 10^{130}$

Number of seconds in 3×10^{12} years $= 10^{20}$

Number of possible events per particle per second $= 10^{20}$

∴ Number of possible events in space and time $= 10^{130+20+20} = 10^{170}$

Probability of Chance Origin of Life

Probability of chance organization of particles into replicating molecule by succession of connected events $= 10^{-450}$

∴ Probability of one replicating molecule arising by chance in all of space and time $= \dfrac{10^{170}}{10^{450}} = 10^{-280} \cong 0.$

Number of Events in Space and Time;
Probability of Chance Origin of Life

ordered combinations. For example, if a system has four components connected linearly, only two (1-2-3-4, 4-3-2-1) of the 24 possible combinations possess really meaningful order. The ratio rapidly decreases as the number of components increases. The more complex and orderly a system is, the more unique it is among its possible competitors. This objection, therefore, misses the point. In the example cited above, only one combination would work. There would be 10^{280} that would not work.

Some might think that, even if the first living cell had to be created, further evolutionary advances could be brought about naturalistically. The complexity of each new subsystem to be added to the living system, however, is at least as complex as the first system. The improbabilities can only increase as the complexity increases. All of which is only another way of saying that, in the present order of things, the Second Law of Thermodynamics makes naturalistic evolution toward higher complexity impossible. No matter how old the earth and universe may be, there has not been enough time for evolution.

Chapter 6
PRACTICAL SCIENTIFIC IMPLICATIONS OF THE CREATION MODEL

The preferred model of origins—whether Creation or Evolution—obviously has religious and social implications. The purpose of this paper, however, is to examine the Creation Model only in terms of its scientific evidences and implications.

If the Creation Model is really valid, then most of the millions of dollars and man-hours being spent on trying to prove or understand evolution are futile. The tremendous effort to "create life in a test tube" is one example. The space program has been promoted mainly on the hope that it might prove evolution. All the efforts to locate non-existent "missing links" between man and an assumed non-human ancestor are also redundant.

If some of the time and money spent on these and other evolution-oriented projects had been spent on creation-oriented research, the returns might well have been more productive. For example, if the topography and ecology of the pre-Flood world could be determined through careful analysis of the world's subsurface geology, and if the hydraulic, volcanic, and tectonic phenomena of the Flood could then be reproduced through computer modeling or other means, it is likely that a more accurate picture could be drawn of the magnitude and location of fossil fuel reserves and ore deposits. It is already evident that such materials are found indiscriminately in rocks of all the geologic "ages," so that the imagined evolutionary history of a region is of no value in such exploration.

In the study of all kinds of systems, both living and non-living, teleology would once again be recognized as a valuable discipline. If things were studied and evaluated in terms of their created purposes, instead of an imaginary history of random and purposeless evolution, a vastly expanded comprehension of the meaning of structure, symbiosis, ecology, and other relationships could be derived, with unlimited economic implications. A return to the perspective of Isaac Newton and other scientific giants of the past (e.g., "thinking God's thoughts after Him") might well result in new scientific insights and discoveries commensurate with those of such men.

In any case, there is potentially much to gain and nothing significant to lose by at least opening scientific thinking to a two-model approach to the evaluation of all scientific data. Academic freedom, civil rights, scientific objectivity, and expanded scientific understanding of the world would all be well served by considering *both* the evolution and creation models in all such studies in the future.

REFERENCES

1. L. Harrison Matthews, "Introduction," *The Origin of Species,* by Charles Darwin (London, J. M. Dent and Sons, Ltd., 1971), p. x.
2. C. Leon Harris, "An Axiomatic Interpretation of the Neo-Darwinian Theory of Evolution," *Perspectives in Biology and Medicine,* Winter 1975, p. 179.
3. Isaac Asimov, "Can Decreasing Entropy Exist in the Universe?" *Science Digest,* May 1973, p. 76.
4. Ilya Prigogine, Gregoire Nicolis, & Agnes Babloyants, "Thermodynamics of Evolution," *Physics Today* (Vol. 25, November 1972), p. 23.
5. Ilya Prigogine, "Can Thermodynamics Explain Biological Order?" *Impact of Science on Society* (Vol. XXIII, No. 3, 1973), p. 169.
6. David Layzer, "The Arrow of Time," *Scientific American* (Vol. 233, December 1975), p. 60.
7. Ibid.

8. Charles J. Smith, "Problems with Entropy in Biology," *Biosystems* (Volume I, 1975), p. 259.

9. Theodosius Dobzhansky, *Genetics and the Origin of Species* (2nd Ed., New York, Columbia University Press, 1951), p. 4.

10. George Gaylord Simpson, *The Major Features of Evolution* (New York, Columbia University Press, 1953), p. 360.

11. David B. Kitts, "Paleontology and Evolutionary Theory," *Evolution* (Vol. 28, September 1974), p. 467.

12. James W. Valentine and Cathryn A. Campbell, "Genetic Regulation and the Fossil Record," *American Scientist* (Vol. 63, November-December, 1975), p. 673.

13. H. D. Hedberg, "The Stratigraphic Panorama," *Bulletin of the Geological Society of America* (Vol. 72, April 1961), p. 499.

14. O. H. Schindewolf, "Comments on Some Stratigraphic Terms," *American Journal of Science,* Volume 255, June 1957, p. 394.

15. C. O. Dunbar, *Historical Geology* (2nd Ed., New York, John Wiley and Sons, Inc., 1960), p. 47.

16. David G. Kitts, "Paleontology and Evolutionary Theory," *Evolution,* Vol. 28, September 1974, p. 466.

17. Ronald R. West, "Paleontology and Uniformitarianism" *Compass,* Vol. 45, May 1968, p. 216.

18. Derek V. Ager, *The Nature of the Stratigraphical Record* (New York, John Wiley and Sons, Inc., 1973), p. 100.

19. K. Hong Chang, "Unconformity-Bounded Stratigraphic Units," *Bulletin,* Geological Society of America, Vol. 86, November 1975, p. 1545.

20. Ibid., p. 1544.

21. Thomas G. Barnes, *Origin and Destiny of the Earth's Magnetic Field* (San Diego, Institute for Creation Research, 1973), p. 25.

22. Melvin A. Cook, "Do Radiological Clocks Need Repair?", *Creation Research Society Quarterly,* Vol. 5, October 1968, p. 70.

23. Henry M. Morris (Ed.), *Scientific Creationism for Public Schools* (San Diego, Institute for Creation Research, 1974), pp. 151-153.

24. Melvin A. Cook, "Where is the Earth's Radiogenic Helium?", *Nature,* Vol. 179, January 26, 1957, p. 213.

25. Henry M. Morris, *The Troubled Waters of Evolution* (San Diego, Creation Life Publishers, 1974), pp. 145-154.

26. Stuart E. Nevins, "Evolution: The Ocean Says No." *Impact Series, ICR Acts and Facts,* Vol. 2, No. 8, October 1973.

27. Dudley J. Whitney, *The Face of the Deep* (New York, Vantage Press, 1955).

28. Melvin A. Cook, *Prehistory and Earth Models* (London, Max Parrish, 1966).

29. Harold S. Slusher, *Critique of Radiometric Dating* (San Diego, Institute for Creation Research, 1973).

30. John C. Whitcomb, Jr., and Henry M. Morris, *The Genesis Flood* Philadelphia Presbyterian and Reformed Publishing Company, 1961).

31. Benjamin F. Allen, "The Geologic Age of the Mississippi River," *Creation Research Society Quarterly,* Vol. 9 (September 1972), pp. 96-114.

32. R. D. Wilson et al., "Natural Marine Oil Seepage," *Science* (Vol. 184), May 24, 1974, pp. 857-865.

33. "Natural Plutonium," *Chemical and Engineering News,* September 20, 1971.

34. Halton Arp. "Observational Paradoxes in Extragalactic Astronomy," *Science,* Vol. 174 (December 17, 1971), pp. 1189-1200.

35. V. A. Hughes and D. Routledge, "An Expanding Ring of Interstellar Gas with Center Close to the Sun," *Astronomical Journal,* Vol. 77, No. 3 (1972), pp. 210-214.
36. R. S. Boekl, "Search for Carbon 14 in Tektites," *Journal of Geophysical Research,* Vol. 77, No. 2 (1972), pp. 367-368.
37. Harold S. Slusher, "Some Astronomical Evidences for a Youthful Solar System," *Creation Research Society Quarterly,* Vol. 8 (June 1971), pp. 55-57.
38. Harold S. Slusher, *Age of the Earth from Some Astronomical Indicators,* Unpublished manuscript.
39. Thomas G. Barnes, "Physics, A Challenge to Geologic Time," *Impact Series 16, ICR Acts and Facts,* Institute for Creation Research, July 1974.
40. Maurice Ewing, J. I. Ewing and M. Talwan, "Sediment Distribution in the Oceans - Mid-Atlantic Ridge," *Bulletin of the Geophysical Society of America,* Vol. 75 (January 1964), pp. 17-36.
41. *Chemical Oceanography,* Ed. by J. P. Riley and G. Skirrow (New York, Academic Press, Vol. 1, 1965), p. 164. See also Harold Camping, "Let the Oceans Speak," *Creation Research Society Quarterly,* Vol. 11, (June 1974), pp. 39-45.

42. Marcel E. Golay, "Reflections of a Communications Engineer", *Analytical Chemistry,* Vol. 33, (June 1961), p. 23.

43. Frank B. Salisbury, "Doubts about the Modern Synthetic Theory of Evolution," *American Biology Teacher,* (September 1971), p. 336.

44. Harold V. Morowitz, "Biological Self-Replicating Systems", *Progress in Theoretical Biology,* Ed. F. M. Snell (New York: Academic Press, 1967), pp 35 ff.

45. James E. Coppedge, *Evolution: Possible or Impossible* (Grand Rapids, Zondervan, 1973), pp. 95-115.

INDEX OF FIGURES

APPENDIX A

This small book covers the scientific case for creation only in an introductory way. It is hoped that the reader will be sufficiently interested and intrigued by the evidence to want to investigate the subject in much greater depth than could be possible in a brief introduction such as this. With this in mind, the following annotated bibliography should prove helpful. The list is not meant to be a complete listing of studies on creationism, since the literature in this field is rapidly growing today, but at least it is representative and comprehensive in relation to topics covered.

All of the books shown are entirely or predominantly scientific in emphasis. There are, of course, many other books dealing with the evolution-creation question in which the orientation is primarily Biblical or philosophical. There are others which are pseudo-creationist but which attempt to compromise with evolutionism or uniformitarianism in varying degrees. None of these are included, since the one purpose of this bibliography is to direct the reader to books which further amplify and document the scientific evidence for strict creationism as presented in this introductory study. The other types of books—those dealing with Biblical creationism and with pseudo-creationism, are more widely known and available already, but there has been a great need for reference material on consistent scientific creationism.

Although the books listed below are from various publishers, the reader may, if he wishes, obtain any or all of them from the publisher of this book (Creation-Life Publishers, P. O. Box 15666, San Diego, California 92115). A complete catalog describing these and other creationist books is available from these publishers on request.

BIBLIOGRAPHY

Barnes, Thomas G., *Origin and Destiny
of the Earth's Magnetic Field*
(San Diego, Institute for Creation
Research, 1976), 64 pp.
   A study by an outstanding physicist and
authority on terrestrial magnetism,
demonstrating that the earth almost certainly was created less than 10,000 years
ago. The decay of the earth's magnetic
field, of all processes, probably most nearly satisfies the necessary uniformitarianism assumptions and so probably
yields the best physical estimate of the
earth's age.

Gish, Duane T., *Evolution? The Fossils
Say NO!* (2nd Ed., San Diego,
Creation-Life Publishers, 1973),
134 pp.
   Dr. Gish, who is Associate Director of
the Institute for Creation Research, has
participated in more formal creation-
evolution debates on university campuses,
than any other man, using the material in
this book with devastating effectiveness.
The most complete documentation in print
of the universal absence of evolutionary

transitional forms in the fossil record, with special attention to the question of supposed evolutionary ancestors of man.

Gish, Duane T., *Speculations and Experiments Related to the Origin of Life (A Critique)* (San Diego, Institute for Creation Research, 1972), 41 pp.

The question of the origin of the first living system in the supposed primordial soup and the various attempts to synthesize life in the laboratory are critically analyzed in this monograph by a man of eminent qualifications. Dr. Gish has a Ph.D. in Biochemistry from the University of California at Berkeley and many years of top-level experience in biomedical and biochemical research. He shows conclusively that life could never be produced from non-life by any natural process or artificial synthesis. It can only be the product of supernatural creation by a living and omniscient Creator.

Howe, George F., Ed., *Speak to the Earth* (Nutley, N.J., Craig Press, 1975), 463 pp.

A collection of 26 studies in creationist geology, originally published by various authors in the *Creation Research Society Quarterly* during the five year period from June 1969 to June 1974. Dr. Howe was Editor of the *Quarterly* during those years, and these papers were selected as significant research contributions supporting creationism and catastrophism in the study of the various earth sciences.

Lammerts, Walter E., Ed., *Why Not Creation?* (Philadelphia, Pa., Presbyterian and Reformed Publ. Co., 1970), 388 pp.

A classified anthology of articles on many different aspects of scientific creationism, originally published in the *Creation Research Society Quarterly* during its first five years, 1964-1968. The editor of this book was also the Society's first president and the *Quarterly's* first editor. Dr. Lammerts is a world-renowned plant geneticist.

Lammerts, Walter E., Ed., *Scientific Studies in Special Creation* (Philadelphia, Presbyterian and Reformed Publ. Co., 1971), 343 pp.

The companion volume to *Why Not Creation?* More studies from the *Creation Research Society Quarterly* for the period 1964-1968. The Creation Research Society is an association of over 500 scientists with post-graduate degrees in one of the natural sciences, all committed to belief in strict creationism, a young earth, and worldwide flood. All fields of natural science are represented in the Society, so it is evident that creationism can be considered compatible with the data in any branch of science.

Morris, Henry M., Ed., *Scientific Creationism* (San Diego, Creation-Life Publishers, 1974), 277 pages.

Probably the most thorough and best-documented recent treatment of all aspects of scientific creationism currently available. Intended as a reference handbook for teachers, it is available in both a general edition and a public school edition, the latter without the chapter on the Biblical doctrine of creation which was included in the general edition. A total of 23 scientists participated in the preparation of this volume, either as writers or consultants.

Morris, Henry M. *The Troubled Waters of Evolution* (San Diego, Creation-Life Publishers, 1975), 217 pp.

A detailed study of the influence and history of evolutionary thought in all areas of education and society, with emphasis upon the increased public awareness of the unscientific nature of evolutionism and the dangers inherent in the current applications of evolutionary thinking to modern world problems. Also includes a thorough discussion of the Second Law of

Thermodynamics and its refutation of evolution as a scientific principle.

Morris, Henry M., and Gish, Duane T., Eds., *The Battle for Creation* (San Diego, Creation-Life Publishers, 1976), 321 pp.
An up-to-date documentation of the modern revival of scientific creationism. Covers the university debates, creation seminars, teachers' workshops, legal developments, public school controversies, scientific confrontations, and other interactions between the creationist scientists and evolutionists during 1974 and 1975. Also includes all the popular and incisive I.C.R. *Impact Series* articles published in the Institute's popular monthly journal *Acts and Facts* during those two years, as well as discussions of the importance of creationism in many areas of life.

Slusher, Harold S., *Critique of Radiometric Dating* (San Diego, Institute for Creation Research, 1973), 46 pp.
A scientific evaluation of the uranium-lead, potassium-argon, radiocarbon, and other geochronometric techniques used in age-dating of geological systems by radioactive elements. Dr. Slusher is a geophysicist and astronomer and shows persuasively that even these methods which have been most widely accepted

among evolutionists and uniformitarians will, when corrected with more reasonable and accurate assumptions, yield very young ages for the earth, far too young for evolution to be feasible.

Whitcomb, John C. and Morris, Henry M., *The Genesis Flood* (Grand Rapids, Baker Book House, 1961), 518 pp.

The book that served as the main catalyst to stimulate the modern revival of scientific creationism. Still contains the most comprehensive and most thoroughly-documented analysis of all the geological and geophysical aspects of the creation-evolution question, with special emphasis on the recency of creation and on the global deluge as the main cause of the earth's great beds of sedimentary rocks and fossils.

THE AUTHOR

Henry M. Morris is Director of the Institute for Creation Research in San Diego, California, and is former president of the Creation Research Society. With a B.S. from Rice University (Civil Engineering) and M.S. and Ph.D. from the University of Minnesota (major in Hydraulics, minors in Geology and Mathematics), Dr. Morris has spent 37 years in scientific research, teaching, and administration. He was Chairman of the Department of Civil Engineering at the Virginia Polytechnic Institute from 1956 to 1970, when he became a co-founder of Christian Heritage College and its Institute for Creation Research. He is author of five books in the fields of hydrology and water resources and seventeen books in the fields of scientific creationism and Christian apologetics.

more significant books for you...
from CLP PUBLISHERS
P. O. Box 15666, San Diego, California 92115

Should Evolution Be Taught?
John N. Moore

A brief treatise on the manner in which evolution should be taught, by Professor of Natural Sciences, John N. Moore, Ed.D. 48 pages, paper.

DINOSAURS: Those Terrible Lizards
Duane T. Gish

At last! A book for young people, profusely illustrated in color, on those intriguing dinosaurs from a creationist perspective. By the author of the best seller *Evolution? The Fossils Say NO!* 9" x 11" Clothbound.

Education for the REAL World
Henry M. Morris

A book every parent, pastor, teacher, and school administrator should read. A comprehensive discussion about the Bible as the basis for all areas of study, and how to insure that you have a Bible-based education in Christian schools, rather than a secular education in a Christian environment. Quality paperback.

Ebla Tablets: SECRETS of a Forgotten City
Clifford Wilson

This book by noted archaeologist, Dr. Clifford Wilson, reveals the secrets of the greatest "find" since the Dead Sea Scrolls. An abundance of clay tablets in a buried city in the Tell Mardikh contain such fascinating information as trade documents referring to the Garden of Eden (Dilmun) as an actual geographic location; and a creation tablet remarkably similar to the Hebrew record — *in writing* more than 2000 years before Christ; discusses the Tower of Babel and much more. 160 pages, paper.

The Passover Plot EXPOSED
Clifford Wilson

Dr. Wilson, who so ably answered von Däniken's absurd speculations in his million-copy best seller *Crash Go The Chariots,* now challenges the confused (but widely accepted) imaginings of Dr. Hugh Schonfield, author of the book (and now movie), *The Passover Plot.* Wilson readily substantiates that the death and resurrection of Jesus was not a *PLOT,* but the greatest *PLAN* of all ages. 224 pages, paper.

Crash Go the Chariots
Clifford Wilson

Newly revised and enlarged, the original book of this title was the near million bestselling answer to von Däniken's theories concerning unexplained happenings and ruins. These revealing answers to mysterious and haunting questions will arouse your curiosity and at the same time provide sensible answers to von Däniken and his often absurd claims. About 156 pages, Paper.

Many Infallible Proofs   *Henry M. Morris*

A comprehensive and systematic handbook written as a survey of the unique truth and authority of biblical Christianity. Contains evidence from science, prophecy, history, internal structure, philosophy and common sense. Complete with questions and answers, an excellent reference for church and home study. 381 pages: Kivar, Cloth.

The Remarkable Birth of Planet Earth
Henry M. Morris

An exciting journey back to our beginnings is in this concise introductory treatment of origins. Covers the amazing order of the universe, early history of all mankind, delusion of evolution, the worldwide flood and many other historical and prophetic confirmations of God's handiwork. 111 pages, Paper.